A Guide to Starting Your Own Business

✑CONVERSATIONS✑
with
JACK & JILL

Tamira K. Webster

ISBN: 1463742533
ISBN-13: 9781463742539
Library of Congress Control Number: 2011912882
CreateSpace, North Charleston, SC

CONTENTS

INTRODUCTION

We all know the story well. It was televised on every station and reported in every newsmagazine around the globe. Tabloids carried the story for months after it happened. I can still remember where I was on that fateful day when I heard the news that Jack and Jill had gone up the hill to fetch a pail of water. Then, without warning, Jack fell down and broke his crown, and poor Jill came tumbling after.

The story didn't end there. Having learned from their public mishap at the hill, Jack and Jill went on to start a successful water bottling business, J & J Sparkling Water Company, which has gone on to gross billions, making it the most lucrative venture ever born out of calamity.

Recently, I sat down with the principals of that company for a friendly one-on-one discussion about the lessons learned along the path to starting their own business.

PART 1

Researching the Idea

Interviewer:
I'm glad you both could take time out of your busy schedules to sit down and speak with me about the skyrocketing success of J & J Sparkling Water.

Jack and Jill:
Our pleasure.

Interviewer:
I guess the first question on everyone's mind is how you two got from what has come to be known as "the incident at the hill" to where you are today.

Jack:
Well, after enduring the embarrassment at the hill, we realized that there had to be a better way to go about getting a drink of water.

Jill:
Plus we didn't want anyone else to have to suffer the same fate that we did.

Jack:
So we started brainstorming and came up with the idea of bottling water.

Jill:
Right. Instead of people having to struggle up that hill just to get one pail of water at a time, we thought wouldn't it be great to bring the water to the people.

Jack:
When we left our small village to go to the city to sell the idea, we realized that not only were there

other companies that had the same idea before us, there were already several brands of bottled water on the shelves of every major grocery and convenience store!

Jill:
Talk about living under a rock! (laughs)

Interviewer:
So what were your first steps toward making your idea a reality?

Jack and Jill:
Research!

Jill:
We needed to understand the water bottling business, so we grabbed every book there was on the subject, spoke with other competitors by joining their trade organization, and attended seminars and trade shows to get up to speed.

Jack:
Not only that, but we also researched the market to determine how many companies were out there and whether there was room for one more water bottling company to enter the arena and make a profit.

We'll return to the interview in a moment, but this is a good place to stop and review several critical points. Keep in mind that when starting your own business, it is essential that you educate yourself on all aspects of how that type of business is run. Research is the key to discovery when starting a successful new venture.

Think about your idea for a new business, and write out your plan for gaining more in-depth knowledge. It doesn't matter if you are starting a catering business, custodial service, computer programming business, restaurant, daycare center, hair salon/barber shop, or the like, the same rule of thumb applies.

Even if you have experience working in a particular field or industry, there is still a lot to be learned about owning and running a business in that same arena. Ask employers, and they will most likely tell you that the vast list of issues that you are responsible for handling when you own a company far exceeds the tasks of those who work specific jobs within the company.

At any given time, there are a myriad of behind-the-scenes decisions that must be made and a variety of responsibilities and obligations that must be handled on a daily basis that require a broader knowledge base than you might expect. You need to be prepared to tackle any entrepreneurial issue that might come up, because you will be the one that others will come to for the answer.

Use this time to create a checklist that includes ways to network within your chosen industry and to see how others are doing what you are trying to do. Become knowledgeable about the market. How many others in your geographical area are doing what you want to do? What do they charge for their product or service? Is there room for you to compete? What books can you read? What seminars can you attend that will help you to start a business that stands out from the rest?

Like J & J Sparkling Water, the success of your business begins with laying a strong foundation that is rooted in research and knowledge.

PART 2

Developing the Idea

Once you have laid the foundation of your business by researching the idea, you can turn your focus toward developing the idea—creating the product or defining the service based on your research.

Let's return to our conversation with Jack and Jill on the subject of creating their product.

Interviewer:
What was the next step for you after you gathered all of your research?

Jill:
We wanted to figure out a way to make our product stand out from the rest, but it's water—how much of a difference can you really hope to achieve?

Jack:
Exactly. We thought of making it flavored water, but there were already several brands of flavored water on the market.

Jill:
We also looked at distinguishing our product with unique packaging options. First, we played with different labeling variations and then different bottle designs, but in the end, a bottle is a bottle no matter how many ways you look at it.

Jack:
So we tried to look ahead to figure out where the bottled water industry was headed instead of where it was currently, and that's when we were able to strike gold.

Jill:
We became one of the first companies to create eco-friendly bottles with labels made from 100 percent recycled paper.

Jack:
We also capitalized on the growing trend toward healthier living by offering vitamin water, which became a source of vitamins and minerals people need on a daily basis.

Jill:
This was key, because it effectively placed us above our competitors. The average consumers could always argue that water is water, whether it's from a spring or out of their tap, but they couldn't deny the fact that tap water does not come with the essential supplement of vitamins and minerals that our product offered.

Jack:
When faced with a decision whether to spend their dollars on our product versus the other products on the shelves...

Jill:
...for something they could get for free...

Jack:
...we provided an added intrinsic value to our product, which tilted consumer spending in our direction.

Jill:
And this distinction gave us the necessary leg up in our marketing effort.

Jack:
True. It's one thing to distinguish a product, but it doesn't help if no one knows that this great new product exists!

Interviewer:
So you're saying that marketing is an important aspect of product development?

Jack and Jill:
Absolutely!

Interviewer:
What was the next step?

Jill:
Once we understood the market and developed the product and the marketing direction, we used that information to assess what it would take to run the business. It was overwhelming at first, because we needed to figure out so many details, like where the business would be located. Were we going to lease a building or buy one? We had to determine the kind of equipment and supplies we would need. Plus, because it was clear that it was going to take more than the two of us to run the business, we had to think about hiring employees.

Jack:
Most importantly, how were we going to pay for it!

Interviewer:
That brings me to my next question. Can you tell us how you went about getting funding for your business?

Jack:
We had some savings set aside, but it was clear that we were going to need more to get us up and running, so once again, we needed to research funding options.

Jill:
We got on the Internet and researched local grants and bank business loans as well as private equity "angel investment" and venture capital firms. We even discussed whether we would go to family and friends to borrow the money.

Jack:
Ultimately, we decided that the best option for us was a combination of savings and loans. Once we determined the kind of business loan we wanted, we discovered that we would have to submit a written business plan to apply.

Jill:
Right. The only problem was that we had no idea what a business plan was! Once again, we needed to research what the plan was and how to get one. When it was all said and done, the business plan turned out to be a life saver.

Jack:
Agreed. The business plan became the foundation and roadmap for our entire company. It forced us to write down our thoughts and ideas for the business in a way that helped us see our plan for product development, marketing, financing, management, and production from an objective point of view.

Jill:
We had all of the research in front of us and all of these thoughts and ideas whirling around in our heads, but it wasn't until we put them down on paper that the business became real and began to take shape.

Jack:
Exactly. We could see areas in the plan that needed more thought, like management, and other areas of the plan that were unrealistic in terms of timing, like production.

Jill:
Basically, the process of writing the plan helped us to fine tune our thinking about the business...

Jack:
...which helped us to avoid costly mistakes in the long run!

Jill:
Like I said, a life saver.

This portion of our conversation with Jack and Jill revealed several key principles that are important to note as you begin developing your product or defining your service.

First and foremost, it is important to find a way to distinguish your product or service from those of your competitors. In a vast market society, it is the only way to not only survive but also to thrive. Think of ways to add value to your product or service. Don't be afraid to glance into the future to see where your industry is headed so that you can "beat them to the punch" getting there! Think outside the box, which is another way of saying don't be afraid to do something radical, something new, something that hasn't been done before!

Once you've come up with your radically brilliant idea for your new product or service, use those attributes to establish a marketing program that highlights the features that will attract the kind of customers you want and need.

Next, narrow your focus to consider what it will take to run your business. What type of supplies or equipment will you need? Where will you get them? Which companies will sell you what you need at the best price?

Where will your business be located? Is this a business that you can run from your home? Will you need to buy or lease commercial space in a building zoned for your type of business?

Who will help you run your business? Is this something that you can do all on your own? Will you need to hire personnel? Is it better to hire them directly, or should you use a staffing agency? Perhaps you can hire independent consultants or contractors to do the work that you require.

Where will you go for financing? Some people choose to start their business using only the money that they have saved. They withdraw from their savings accounts, borrow against their 401(k) plans, or take out equity loans on their homes. Other business owners who prefer not to use their own money choose traditional bank lending.

Depending on the type of business, you may prefer to approach investors to finance your business start-up costs. Just as Jack and Jill discovered, investors can range from venture capital firms to private equity or "angel investors." These options require that you be willing to part with a percentage of the ownership in your business in exchange for funding, but you are not obligated to pay back the money invested.

You could even choose to ask a family member or friend to invest or loan money to your business. Grants through state and local programs are available for certain types of businesses operating in certain geographical areas but may be limited in terms of the amount of funding available. Ultimately, you will need to decide the type of funding that will be the best fit for you and your business.

Once you have researched the product, market, and financing, you are ready to put your thoughts and research down on paper. It's important to map out the future of your business by creating a business plan that captures what you will need to start and sustain the business for years to come.

The business plan serves as a reference point to refer to when you feel that you've lost your way as well as a barometer to track your progress and success. It's a document that changes, because as your business grows and becomes more and more profitable, you will want to add new strategies and creative ways to stay on top.

Take this opportunity to jot down your ideas and begin the process of bringing your product or service to life!

PART 3

Handling the Business Side

Interviewer:
Once you developed the product by determining the look and taste of the ideal bottle of water, was it just a matter of placing the bottles on retail shelves?

Jack:
Not even close!

Jill:
We learned that there were still many other tasks that needed to be done before we could officially open our doors for business, so to speak.

Jack:
First, we had to open a business checking account, which we couldn't do until we filed articles of incorporation papers with the state.

Jill:
There were also other business filings with the state that had to be handled, such as obtaining a seller's permit and business tax licenses.

Jack:
Once we came up with the company name and logo that would appear on the bottles, we needed to file for trademark registration to protect our rights to the name and design.

Jill:
We didn't have a lot of money to start with, so we did most of the filings ourselves, using the Internet and books we found in the library. For the remaining

tasks we needed help with, we hired an attorney and an accountant.

Just as Jack and Jill discovered, there are a myriad of t's to cross and i's to dot when starting your own business. The business side of business is often what business owners dread most! Admittedly, tasks like filing incorporation papers with the state are not as fun, creative, or glamorous as developing your product or service, decorating your space, or planning your big opening, but they are nevertheless just as important.

Do you have a business support group in place? Have you chosen a banking institution, an accountant, an attorney and/or other business professionals specific to your industry who can help you navigate the maze of business filings and paperwork? Remember, even if you are handling most of the filings on your own, you never know when it might be useful to have professionals at your disposal when you need them to answer questions.

Have you decided under which type of legal business entity you will operate? Will your business operate as a sole proprietorship, a general partnership, a limited partnership, a C or S corporation, or a limited liability company? Each type of entity carries distinguishable characteristics from legal and tax perspectives that should be considered when forming your business. While it is advisable that you consult your tax professional and/or attorney to assist with choosing the entity that best suits your particular business, you can also search the Internet and your local library or bookstore for the differences between these entities and the filing requirements in your state.

Keep in mind that if you choose to incorporate your business, you will need to file with the Securities Exchange Commission should you later decide to distribute shares of your business in the form of stocks as a means of creating operating capital. Consulting your business support group is advisable before undertaking this method of financing.

In addition to establishing a legal entity, you should research or ask your attorney or tax professional the extent to which your state requires licenses, permits, and/or insurance policies to be obtained before starting your business such as business tax licenses, seller's permits, errors and omissions insurance, and the like. If you will be hiring employees, you'll need to determine the appropriate tax and employer identification documentation to be filed.

Once you have taken care of the licenses and business structure, you want to ensure that your intellectual property rights are protected. Intellectual property rights consist of exclusive legal rights afforded to individuals for creation of intangible works such as music, inventions, art, words, phrases, designs, symbols, etc. Typically, these rights can be covered under copyright, trademark, and/or patent law. While your legal professional is your best resource to help you to navigate these issues, you can always research the distinctions on the Internet or in your local library or bookstore.

You should begin creating your checklist to ensure that all aspects of your company's business are in place when the time comes. For those who are still trying to determine what kind of business to start, we return to our interview for some helpful tips.

PART 4

Starting Your Own Business

Interviewer:
You obviously had a personal stake in wanting to refine the water retrieval business, but what would you say to those who know they want to start a business but have no idea about what kind of business to start?

Jill:
I think the best approach is to start by finding something that you're good at or something in which you have a vested interest.

Jack:
I agree. Sometimes the best hobbies can become the most profitable of businesses. Look at your talents and skill sets, and try turning those into viable business ideas.

Jill:
For example, if you love to cook or bake, and you're always being praised by friends, family, and colleagues about how much of a wonderful cook you are, you may want to consider starting your own bakery or home catering business.

Jack:
Or if you're really good at fixing things or at auto repair, you could start your own fix-it shop, auto body shop, or mechanic's garage.

Jill:
Take it from us—it helps to be passionate about your business, because it's going to take up a huge amount of your time. When you're already good at it or if it's something that you enjoy doing at the

outset, it puts you that much closer to maximizing your potential for success!

To further illustrate the point, let's take a look at several hobbies, talents, and skill sets and the business ideas we can come up with for each. For example, if you have natural design skills and are good at looking at an empty space and imagining lots of ways to decorate it in terms of furnishings, color schemes, and the like, you could help people who have purchased new homes or those who want to redecorate their home by starting an interior decorating firm. You could assist those interested in selling their homes by offering home staging services (where you eliminate clutter and make the space aesthetically appealing to prospective buyers).

If you are organized and pride yourself on keeping your home or office space tidy, and you derive a sense of accomplishment in doing so, you may want to consider starting a commercial or residential cleaning business.

Organization skills and a customer-friendly attitude also make for an ideal home-based virtual/personal assistant business or a concierge/lifestyle management business. You can answer phones, handle typing, make appointments, set up conference calls, run errands, process mail, schedule meetings, make reservations, and handle travel arrangements for clients who are in need of these services but are unable to hire a full-time employee to handle them.

If you enjoy being outside and have a natural affection for flora and fauna, with the green thumb and design skills to match, you might consider starting a floral shop, greenhouse, or landscaping and design business.

If you are organized, like to shop, and you enjoy helping others, you can start a personal shopping or image consulting firm. You can help those with no time to focus on their personal or professional appearance as well as help those who do not know how to create the perfect personal and professional image for themselves.

With the same skill set, you could start an event planning business (helping your clients handle the logistics of creating the ideal party, convention, wedding, meeting or other event). If you have a natural eye for capturing the event on film, you can start a photography or videography shop.

These are but a few examples of possible business ideas, but as you can see, the possibilities are endless. Take a moment to brainstorm and jot down the activities that you enjoy along with skills and talents that you have. Your new business idea is just on the horizon. The possibilities are as far-reaching as your imagination will take you!

Now that you have an idea about what kind of business you might start, let's use what you've learned thus far to get it up and running. We'll use one of the businesses referenced earlier as an example.

Virtual Assistant/Personal Concierge

You know that to start this type of business, you need to first research the idea. One of the best ways to do this is to speak with others who are already running similar businesses. Research whether there are professional organizations that you can join. Attend conferences for purposes of networking and gaining knowledge about how to stay competitive in the virtual assistant (VA) or personal concierge (PC) space. Find out how many other VA or PC businesses exist in your general area. How many have an online presence? What do they charge for their services? How can you make your business stand out from the rest? What services can you offer that are not currently being offered by other VA or PC businesses?

Now it's time to further distinguish your services in the VA/PC marketplace. Once you've done your research, you will have a better idea of the kinds of services that other companies are offering to clients. Brainstorm customer-friendly touches that you can add to your list of services that others may not offer. Take a long view into the future, anticipate the direction that the VA/PC business is heading, and make decisions that will get you there ahead of the competition!

Next, identify how you can reach your target clientele. How will you attract new clients to your business? Marketing and networking are key for this type of business. If you were an assistant in your previous job, it is easy to contact your past colleagues and ask for referral business.

You can visit local area businesses, meet with the owners or office managers, and share your VA services with them so that they keep you in mind when work cannot be handled in-house. You can set up appointments with boutique hotels in your area that may not offer concierge services but may be interested in partnering with you to provide their guests with services exclusively through your business.

Marketing via the Internet and social media sites should also be incorporated into your overall marketing plan. Word-of-mouth marketing of your services through social media alone can increase your potential client base significantly.

Now narrow your focus to consider what it will take to run your business. What types of supplies or equipment will you need? You will likely need a computer with email and Internet access, a printer, a multiline telephone, and a post office mailing address that you can use to receive client mail. A toll-free number will widen your geographic reach.

Next, turn to what it will take to operate your business. Will you maintain a home-based business, or will you want to expand into leased space? Initially, it may be beneficial to run this type of business out of your home to keep costs down. The good news is that this is a business with relatively low start-up costs that could be run out of your home for the long haul. You could even set it up to have more of an Internet presence, which adds to the virtual nature of the business without adding much over-head. If you decide over time to expand into the brick-and-mortar aspects of the business, you can always buy or lease a space at that time.

Who will help you run your business? Is this some-thing that you can do all on your own? You can, at least initially. Once you build a healthy clientele, you can determine the extent to which you want to hire additional personnel. For this type of business, it may be more convenient to use a temporary staff-ing agency as opposed to hiring additional person-nel directly.

How will you finance your business? Because the start-up costs required for this type of business are low, it can be financed on a shoestring budget. You could choose to use your savings or borrow from your 401(k) plan. If you've recently left your job and were given a severance package, you may choose to use those funds to get your business up and running. You could even borrow money from friends and family.

After determining the type of funding you will use, you can create your business plan. Taking all of the information gathered thus far about your business and putting it on paper will create the foundation necessary to support the future growth and suc-cess of your business.

Once your services are properly researched and developed and your business plan is in place, you can turn to the business side. You will want to hire an accountant and an attorney to ensure that your business entity is properly set up from a legal and tax perspective. An accountant can discuss with you the aspects of federal, state, and local tax costs and requirements to which your business will need to adhere.

An attorney can discuss with you applicable licensing requirements and offer guidance to determine whether you want your business to be a sole proprietorship or a partnership with another party, and whether it is beneficial to incorporate or establish a limited liability company. The attorney may also assist with drafting service agreements that you may require or in protecting your intellectual property rights (such as filing a trademark registration for your company name and/or logo).

Once you have successfully handled the business side, you are ready to open your doors for business!

PART 5

Encouragement for the Journey

Interviewer:
What advice would you want to give to others who are trying to start their own business?

Jill:
I think it's important to see obstacles as opportunities. If we had stopped at the incident on the hill, we wouldn't be where we are today. Was it an embarrassing obstacle? Yes, but we turned it into an opportunity for success, and that's all that matters at the end of the day.

Jack:
Exactly. Business is nothing if not a succession of obstacles along the path to success. At any point, you have the option to turn around and go back to where you came from, because the obstacles are too much to bear, or you can stay on the journey, knowing that success is around the corner.

Jill:
Let's be clear that it is not financial success that we speak of, though that's important. However, because people count success in many ways, it is important to establish from the beginning that you will count yourself among the successful even if you never make a bit of profit. Why? Because you have succeeded in doing what many wish they could do but have not the guts to try, and that is starting your own business.

Jack:
Success comes at the point when you've opened your doors for business. After that, your business, like ours, becomes subject to the whims of commerce.

It can rise and fall for reasons that are completely out of your control, but nothing can ever take away the feeling that comes from knowing that your business exists, not just on paper or in your dreams, but in reality, and you are the reason that it does.

Jill:
Therein lies the epitome of success!

Truer words were never spoken. When measuring success, it is important to realize that once you enter your business into the realm of reality, it will be subjected to outside forces and elements. Competition, a dry market, an oversaturated market, a recession, unemployment, and new technology, among other things, may all affect the success of your newly formed business. However, if your business brings you a sense of purpose, passion, and fulfillment, I encourage you to throw your hat in the ring and play the game. Take a chance on your business idea. Take a chance on yourself. You may beat reality at its own game and come out on top with a personal and financial victory, but you'll never know unless you try, so enjoy the journey!

APPENDIX

NEW BUSINESS BRAINSTORMING SHEET

List your skills and talents:

List your hobbies and interests:

List what you like about each skill, talent, hobby, and interest:

List the characteristics you would like your ideal business to have (e.g., creativity, travel, autonomy, flexibility, outdoors, variety):

List the kinds of businesses that interest you:

Which of your talents, skills, hobbies, or interests would you like to do for a living?

Which kind of business would you prefer to start, a product-based business or a service-based business?

TOP TWENTY SERVICE-BASED BUSINESS IDEAS

The dream of starting your own business may come easier than the task of figuring out what kind of business to start. Below is a list of twenty easy to start service-based businesses that can get you up and running in no time. From arts, crafts and food service to commercial, business and personal services, the list below can help you use your skills, talents and abilities to chart the path toward making your dream of starting a business a reality.

Residential/Commercial Services

Landscaping Consultant

Who: Anyone with a love for flora and fauna (and the "green thumb" to match), coupled with a talent to design open outdoor spaces.

What: Landscaping is the profession of designing or creating gardens or enhancing the land, particularly around the exterior of residential and commercial buildings, by altering its shape and size by means of planting and maintaining trees, shrubs, flowers, and grass. In addition, landscapers handle the installation of outdoor lighting as well as lay foundations for the creation of waterfalls, walkways, patios, decks, bench seating, and the like.

When: Summer months are the busiest, given the outdoor nature of the business.

Where: Exteriors of neighborhood yards, palatial estates, schools, parks, and golf courses, as well as commercial building courtyards and grounds.

How: Start by offering to design some exteriors at no cost until you have a variety of examples for a portfolio. Approach homeowners, state/municipal agencies, educational institutions, and corporate clients by showing them your portfolio.

Interior Decorator

Who: Anyone with natural design skills capable of looking at an empty space and imagining ways to decorate it in terms of adding furnishings, color schemes, and the like to convey a particular style or theme.

What: Interior decorating is the art and process of planning and designing the interior furnishings and decorations of a room or building to achieve a particular look, feel, style, or theme.

When: This is a year-round business.

Where: Interiors including the kitchen, bathroom, nursery, den, office, living area, or bedroom of any residence as well as commercial building common areas, reception areas, lobbies, offices, conference, and break rooms.

How: Start by offering to design some interiors at no cost until you have a variety of examples for a portfolio. Approach homeowners, new home construction companies, corporate clients, doctors' offices, hotel chains, hair salons, law firms, restaurants, art galleries, spas, museums and other businesses by showing them your portfolio.

Home Staging Consultant

Who: Anyone with the ability to look at a home and its features and bring out the "diamond in the rough" by accenting the positive aspects of the home and downplaying the negative to increase the perceived home value and accelerate a purchase by potential buyers.

What: Home staging is the practice of readying a home for sale by making it look more appealing to potential buyers. During this process, the stager will typically remove the homeowner's personal decorating touches and tone down unattractive property features (or improve upon them), while highlighting the more positive attributes of the home to make the home appear more appealing to the personal tastes of a wider variety of potential buyers.

When: This is a year-round business.

Where: Wherever there are real estate properties (new and old) for sale.

How: Start by establishing a network of potential clients by creating relationships with new home construction companies who may hire you to stage model homes for sale, real estate agents who may hire you to help with the resale of their listed properties, and individual homeowners who are in the market to sell. Attend open houses of homes for resale and new home communities to establish contact and offer your services at competitive rates. Create a portfolio of your work to use as a calling card for future clients.

Cleaning Consultant

Who: Anyone who has a penchant for cleanliness, along with the patience and skill to match, and derives a sense of pride, accomplishment, and satisfaction in doing so.

What: Cleaning and maintaining the cleanliness of the interior rooms of any residential or commercial building; includes washing and cleaning windows, vacuuming and cleaning carpets, sweeping, mopping, waxing/buffing floors, dusting and polishing furniture, and emptying garbage containers.

When: This is a year-round business.

Where: Interiors including the kitchen, bathroom, nursery, den, office, living area, or bedroom of any residence as well as commercial building common areas, reception areas, lobbies, offices, and conference and break rooms.

How: Network in your current social circle to generate leads on new business and increase the potential for word-of-mouth referrals. Approach homeowners, corporate clients, doctors' offices, hotel chains, hair salons, law offices, restaurants, art galleries, spas, museums, apartment buildings, and other businesses with a list of services that are offered at competitive rates.

Personal Services

Virtual Assistant (VA)

Who: Anyone with an attitude geared toward friendly customer service who is organized, detail oriented, able to multitask, and enjoys helping others maintain a sense of organization and professionalism.

What: A virtual assistant works independently, providing clients with administrative or personal support and assistance remotely (or virtually), usually operating as a home-based business. Services can include answering phones, typing, setting appointments, running errands, processing mail, scheduling meetings and conference calls, making reservations, and handling travel arrangements for clients who are in need of these services but are unable to hire a full-time employee to handle them.

When: This is a year-round business.

Where: Services are typically performed from home but can be performed from any location.

How: Network in your current social circle to gen-
        erate leads on possible new business and
        increase the potential for word-of-mouth
        referrals. Potential clients include corpo-
        rate clients, doctors' offices, law offices,
        single parents, entertainers, authors, politi-
        cians, and sports figures.

Personal Concierge (PC)

Who: Anyone with an attitude geared toward
        friendly customer service who is organized,
        detail oriented, able to multitask, and
        enjoys working independently as a facili-
        tator and coordinator in addressing the
        needs of others.

What: A personal concierge connects clients
        with high-level service providers, facili-
        tates completion of requested tasks, and
        offers access to valuable information
        using established contacts and cultivated
        relationships in various industries. The con-
        cierge business is designed to help clients
        alleviate the stress and time associated
        with having to complete everyday tasks
        such as making dining reservations, coor-
        dinating child and pet care, and arrang-
        ing pick-up services for dry cleaning, mail,
        and deliveries. A personal concierge may
        also handle more lavish requests such
        as arranging VIP tours, travel and trans-
        portation, opening night ballet, opera or
        theater tickets, prime seats at a sporting
        event, and access to charity galas and
        film premieres.

When: This is a year-round business.

Where: Services may be performed from home or any other desired location.

How: Network in and expand upon your current social circle to begin establishing contacts and building relationships with a variety of businesses that are connected to the services you intend to provide. Once you have your strategic alliances in place, begin networking within your circle to generate leads on possible new clients and increase the potential for word-of-mouth referrals.

Image Consultant

Who: Anyone with an ability to assess and improve upon a person's outward appearance and impression and who enjoys helping people feel and look their best.

What: Image consulting is the act of assessing a person's outward appearance as well as nonverbal and verbal communications in an effort to improve the person's overall projected image. Consultants may make suggestions regarding wardrobe choices, hair color, cut and style, and skin care as well as providing etiquette tips and advice. Consultants may also offer voice coaching along with assertiveness exercises and training.

When: This is a year-round business.

Where: Consultants may lease space, work from home, or travel to clients and meet them at their homes or place of business.

How: Network in and expand upon your current social circle to establish contacts and build relationships with potential strategic partners that you can use as referral business for clients. It is a good idea to have access to several clothing boutiques and key specialists such as food, fitness and vocal coaches as well as hair and makeup professionals. Once you have your alliances in place, network within your circle to generate leads on possible new clients and increase the potential for word-of-mouth referrals.

Event Planner

Who: Anyone with organizational, time management, problem-solving, multitasking skills and who enjoys throwing a good party!

What: Event planners help clients handle the logistics of creating the ideal party, convention, wedding, meeting, grand opening, festival, fundraiser, or other event. Event planners oversee all aspects of planning and implementation, which can include details such as researching and booking the venue, creating the theme and design for the event space, food and beverage service, seating, guest lists, lighting, decorations, audio/visual, and entertainment.

When: This is a year-round business.

Where: Event planners may work from home or lease space in a commercial or office building.

How: Network in and expand upon your current social circle to establish contacts and build relationships with potential strategic partners such as florists, hotel managers, caterers, musicians and supply companies. Use your networking circle to generate leads on possible new clients and increase the potential for word-of-mouth referrals. Offer to oversee the event planning for a few of your family members and friends at no charge to build your portfolio so that you can show future clientele samples of your work.

Travel Coordinator

Who: Anyone with a love for travel and the desire to make travel plans and arrangements for others.

What: A travel coordinator uses travel search engines and sites to research, plan, and coordinate the best travel arrangements for clients at the lowest costs, thereby saving their clients time, money, and needless frustration. Services can specialize in types of travel such as cruises, honeymoons, spa retreats, and safari excursions.

When: This is a year-round business.

Where: You can easily operate a travel coordinator business from home.

How: Start by networking in your current social circle to attract new clients and increase the potential for word-of-mouth referrals.

Photographer/Videographer

Who: Anyone with an eye for capturing the moment in pictures or on video.

What: This type of business allows you to focus your artistic and creative talents on capturing the moment by photographing or videotaping special occasions: weddings, religious ceremonies, birthday parties, family portraits, graduation ceremonies, baby pictures, and everything in between.

When: This is a year-round business, but the busiest season is typically the summer, due to the many graduation ceremonies and weddings that take place during summer months.

Where: Your business can be operated from home, or you may buy or lease commercial space to use as your studio.

How: Start by offering to photograph or videotape functions for family and friends at no cost, and use each gathering as an opportunity to showcase your talents to new prospective clients and create a portfolio of your work. Attend bridal shows and expos to showcase your portfolio of previous work and generate new business. Continue networking in your current social circle to generate leads on new clients and increase the potential for word-of-mouth referrals.

Pet Daycare and Grooming Spa

Who: Anyone with a love for animals who enjoys caring for the pets of others.

What: Keep and care for the pets of your customers while they are away from home (traveling for business or vacation) or during the day while at work. Services can include feeding, walking, playing, grooming, and dog training as well as pick-up and drop-off services.

When: This is a year-round business.

Where: You can have an on-site, home-based business, lease or buy commercial space, or operate a mobile business.

How: Network in your current social circle to increase the potential for word-of-mouth business. Advertise in the surrounding neighborhood to homeowners and area businesses such as pet stores. Hand out flyers at dog walking parks and pet adoption locations. Offer incentives such as "first grooming free" deals to attract new customers, cultivate customer loyalty, and encourage referrals and repeat business.

Business Services

Web Designer

Who: Anyone who is artistically creative and possesses computer graphic art software skills.

What: Web design is the art and process of creating eye-catching, compelling web pages, websites, banner ads, and other web marketing and advertising materials for purposes of highlighting the products and services of large and small businesses.

When: This is a year-round business.

Where: Web designers typically work from home.

How: Start by networking in your current social circle to generate leads on possible new business and increase the potential for word-of-mouth referrals. Create samples of your web designs to attract potential clients such as corporate clients, doctors' offices, hotel chains, restaurants, art galleries, spas, museums and other businesses in need of web design services.

Graphic Artist

Who: Anyone with natural art and design skills capable of creating compelling marketing and advertising materials for large and small businesses.

What: Graphic artists design the style, look, and feel of concept drawings used for packaging, signage, book covers, print ads, business cards, and other marketing and advertising materials in order to capture the attention of the consumer and increase sales of the product or service.

When: This is a year-round business.

Where: Graphic artists may work from home or lease or buy commercial space.

How: Start by networking in your current social circle to generate leads on possible new business and increase the potential for word-of-mouth referrals. Create samples of your designs to attract potential clients such as corporate clients, doctors' offices, hotel chains, hair salons, restaurants, art galleries, spas, museums and other businesses in need of graphic design services.

Computer Tech Support

Who: Anyone with computer repair and technical skills who is patient with a friendly, customer-service attitude.

What: Computer tech support is the process of troubleshooting technical problems with hardware and software applications for purposes of making the computer operational again. Troubleshooting services can take place in person, over the phone, or online.

When: This is a year-round business.

Where: This business can be operated as a telephone-supported, home-based business, can be operated from leased commercial space, or can be provided by traveling to the client's home or business location.

How: Network in your current social circle to gen-
          erate leads on possible new business and
          increase the potential for word-of-mouth
          referrals. Advertise your services to home-
          owners, corporate clients, doctors' offices,
          schools, law offices, apartment building
          residents, and other local businesses.

Auto Spa

Who: Anyone with automotive repair skills and a
          love for cars.

What: Auto spa services can include car wash,
          repair, servicing, and detailing and can
          include areas of specialization such as
          collision repair and paint jobs. Services can
          also include auto pick-up and drop-off for
          corporate clients.

When: This is a year-round business.

Where: Owners typically operate out of a leased
          space.

How: Network in your current social circle to
          increase the potential for word-of-mouth
          business. Advertise in the surround-
          ing neighborhood to homeowners and
          area businesses. Offer incentives such
          as a free car wash or oil change day to
          attract new customers, cultivate cus-
          tomer loyalty, and encourage repeat
          business.

Arts and Crafts Services

Gift Basket Consultant

Who: Anyone with a natural flare for creativity who enjoys giving "the perfect gift."

What: Create baskets filled with gifts themed for any occasion: weddings, baby showers, birthdays, retirements, promotions, graduations, and every holiday in between.

When: This is a year-round business with high volume during the holiday season.

Where: Owners typically work from home initially but may also lease retail space in the case of high-volume business.

How: Start by creating a sales brochure of your gift basket designs and themes to show to prospective new customers. Be sure to give your baskets as gifts to your neighbors, family, and friends as your personal calling card. Attend gift shows and expos to showcase your work and generate new business. Continue networking in your current social circle to generate leads on new customers and increase the potential for word-of-mouth referrals.

Floral Arrangement Consultant

Who: Anyone who loves plants and flowers with the creative touch to match.

What: Floral arrangers create plants and flowers in different designs for occasions such as weddings, birthdays, retirement, promotions, holidays, sympathy, get well, and everything in between.

When: This is a year-round business.

Where: Owners typically work from home initially but may also lease a retail space in the case of high-volume business.

How: Start by creating a sales brochure of your floral arrangements to show to prospective new customers. Be sure to give your floral arrangements to your neighbors, family, and friends as your personal calling card. Attend bridal shows and expos to showcase your work and generate new business. Continue networking in your current social circle to generate leads on new customers and increase the potential for word-of-mouth referrals.

Scrapbooking Consultant

Who: Anyone with natural organization and design skills and a love for helping people memorialize special occasions.

What: Scrapbooking is the art of organizing and preserving personal family history in the form of pictures, memorabilia, artwork, written works, and collectibles in an album creatively designed in layout and form to memorialize family events and occasions. Services can include teaching by means of individual or group instruction, digital scrapbooking on computer, and scrapbooking supply sales, as well as specialized order-based services.

When: This is a year-round business.

Where: This is primarily a home-based business, but if the emphasis is on supply sales, a leased space may be required, depending on volume and stock.

How: Start by networking in your current social circle to attract new clients and increase the potential for word-of-mouth referrals.

Food Services

Caterer

Who: Anyone who enjoys cooking for large groups of people and is skilled at creating tasty cuisine.

What: Caterers specialize in preparing and providing food and beverage services for large and small events: business meetings, conferences, weddings, birthday parties, grand openings, fundraisers, and other social and corporate functions.

When: This is a year-round business.

Where: Though a caterer can operate as a home-based business initially, as business begins to grow, it may become necessary to relocate operations to larger, leased premises.

How: Start by offering to cater functions for family and friends at no cost using each gathering as an opportunity to showcase your menu items to prospective clients. Continue networking in your current social circle to generate leads on possible new business opportunities and increase the potential for word-of-mouth referrals.

Cake/Cupcake Baker

Who: Anyone who enjoys baking and is skilled at creating delicious cakes and cupcakes.

What: Offer an assortment of cakes and cupcakes for parties, weddings, and business meetings or to grocery stores, bakeries, and restaurants.

When: This is a year-round business.

Where: You can operate this type of business from home, or you can open a walk-in or drive-thru dessert bakery by leasing or buying a commercial space.

How: Start by offering your baked goods at functions for family and friends at no cost using each gathering as an opportunity to showcase your cakes and cupcake varieties to prospective clients. Create mini cakes and cupcakes as samples, and take them to area businesses to generate awareness for your product and increase the potential for word-of-mouth referrals.

NEW BUSINESS CHECKLIST

1. Researching the Idea

    ✓ Check to see how many other companies in your geographical area are running the same type of business.
    ✓ What do they charge for their products or services?
    ✓ Is there room for you to compete?
    ✓ What books can you read to learn about your chosen industry?
    ✓ What seminars can you attend that will help you start a business that stands out from the rest?
    ✓ What trade organizations can you join in order to begin networking within your chosen industry?

2. Developing the Idea

    ✓ Brainstorm ways to distinguish your product or service from your competitors.
    ✓ How can you add value to your product or service?
    ✓ What are the future trends of your chosen industry?
    ✓ How will you market your product or service?
    ✓ What type of supplies or equipment will you need for your business?
    ✓ Which suppliers will sell you what you need at the best price?
    ✓ Where will your business be located?
    ✓ Is this a business that you can operate from your home?

✓ Will you need to buy or lease commercial space in a building zoned for your type of business?

✓ Can you operate this type of business on your own?

✓ Who will help you run your business?

✓ Will you need to hire additional personnel?

✓ Is it better to hire your employees directly, use a temporary staffing agency, or hire independent consultants or contractors?

✓ How will you finance your business (savings, 401(k), home equity, investors, bank loans, grants, etc.)?

3. Handling the Business Side

✓ Have you chosen a banking institution, an accountant, an attorney, and/or other business professionals specific to your industry to help support your business?

✓ Which type of legal entity will your business operate under (e.g., sole proprietorship, general partnership, limited partnership, C or S corporation, or limited liability company)?

✓ Have you applied for patent, copyright, and/or trademark protection to safeguard the intellectual property rights of your business?

✓ Have you obtained any required state or local business licenses and/or permits?

✓ Have you obtained your federal tax identification number, also referred to as an employer identification number (EIN)?

✓ Have you obtained the proper insurance for your business (e.g., errors and omissions, Workers Compensation, professional liability, etc.)?

SAMPLE BUSINESS PLAN

A good business plan contains several key components including a title page, table of contents, company description, product description, marketing plan, competitive analysis, organizational plan, operating plan, financial plan, contingency plan and appendix, where applicable. The following sample is a product-based business plan for a fictitious greeting card company, which illustrates the kind of information that is typically included within each of these sections.

ABC E-Card Company

Business Plan

TABLE OF CONTENTS

COMPANY DESCRIPTION

ABC E-Card Company, a company formed as an incorporated entity in the State of California, has determined that today's consumer is in search of the personal touch. Capitalizing on the hundreds of million e-cards sent worldwide each year, ABC E-Card Company seeks to take electronic card giving to the next level. With the evolution of social networking, ABC E-Card Company plans to merge the e-card revolution so that it is available at the touch of a screen within social networking sites and mobile applications.

Society is changing, and now more than ever people are attempting to keep in touch in as many ways possible. Establishing, maintaining, and enhancing family relationships and friendships are of widespread importance.

Helping people establish, maintain, and enhance interpersonal relationships is this company's goal with each unique line of e-cards that we publish. Whether it is a card declaring love in a unique way or a card that offers help in discussing those difficult to phrase feelings, ABC e-cards will always strive to be a step ahead of the rest.

PRODUCT DESCRIPTION

ABC e-cards are available in 2-D, 3-D and 4-D options. They include a level of personalization that is unrivaled in the industry in that the consumer can include a filmed version of the personal greeting to be included as part of the greeting card sentiment.

The cards are presented in high-definition with sur-round sound (where available), appear as mini movies on the recipient's social networking pages, and can be retrieved and viewed using the media of the recipient's choosing.

Proprietary Advantage

While no one entity can have a proprietary advan-tage in the idea itself, we nevertheless enjoy a proprietary advantage in the form of a copyright in each card created by our company as well as a patent in the e-card technology used to create each mini movie. Likewise, we will exclusively own the name of this line of e-cards in the form of a fed-erally registered trademark.

Future Product

Although this business plan is specifically geared toward start-up capital and funding for our first line of e-cards, the following future endeavors and prospective products are currently in the develop-mental stages.

A. Tween E-cards

Tween will be our second line of e-cards designed specifically for the nine to twelve year-old demo-graphic. This line will use the same patented technology for creating mini movie e-cards that can be shared between tweens using their established social networking pages and mobile media.

B. Gaming E-cards

Gaming will be our third line of e-cards that, as the name suggests, will give the sender an opportunity to customize social media games with greeting card sentiments. It presents the recipient with a keepsake while conveying fun and quirky sentiments on the inside.

C. Video E-cards

These e-cards will allow the sender to serenade the recipient in a video concert context. Using the established patented technology, the videos will be presented in high-definition and surround sound and can be sent using any media application and to all social networking sites.

MARKETING PLAN

a. MARKET ANALYSIS

1. Who Will Buy

We recognize that traditionally, a large percentage of cards have been purchased by women. Nevertheless, through this line of greeting cards, we are attempting to include potential male buyers within our target market. To that end, we conducted an all-male, fifty-person survey, in which almost half (42%) of the respondents reported that they buy cards to help them to communicate feelings or to resolve disagreements with family members or friends. Our greeting cards transcend all races, ethnic backgrounds, and socioeconomic levels. Therefore, our target audience will be every-one between the ages of nine and fifty-five.

2. Why They Buy

We anticipate that our target audience will pur-chase our product as an attempt to communicate feelings in a fun, new, and creative way. Out of one hundred people surveyed, 51 percent reported that they enjoy using social media to communi-cate with friends and family. Sixty-three (63%) per-cent of those surveyed reported that they would enjoy an opportunity to send personalized e-cards using their social networking and new media gadgets.

3. Industry Trends

Trends in the greeting card industry vary, but with the emergence and rise of e-card websites, the overall focus is headed toward giving consum-ers more of the kinds of cards they want using the media they want to use to send them. With this in mind, the goal of our Creative Development department is to continuously research and create fresh new material to be added to and included with the initial e-card line.

4. Market Size

The e-card card market is steadily rising. Our com-pany expects to fall squarely within the market share of the industry that e-card companies cur-rently possess. Capitalizing on our unique product features and distribution channels, we realistically hope to obtain .01 percent of the total greeting card market.

5. Pricing Strategy

Our e-cards are competitively priced at $1.99 retail. Our price is based on cards currently existing in the market, which range in price from $.99 to $3.00, with the average card retailing at approximately $1.50. We carefully considered the cost of those cards that, not unlike our own, offered some unique aspect, thereby justifying a position above the industry average.

b. MARKETING STRATEGY

1. Distribution Strategy

Because of the uniqueness of our product, we believe that it is more advantageous to seek out distribution channels that are unique yet wholly accessible to our target market. With this in mind, we were able to avoid the traditional distribution channels generally found within the greeting card industry and focus on the nontraditional, while maintaining high accessibility to our target market.

Traditionally, greeting cards were found in greeting card retail stores. Today, however, most greeting cards are sold in specialty stores, including chain drug stores, discount stores and supermarkets. Greeting card sales in other alternative channels of distribution, such as car wash establishments, coffee houses, college campuses, and the like, are also popular. Our strategy for distribution is to initially stay away from traditional greeting card brick-and-mortar specialty stores to attain more visibility among our mobile and online target audience.

Our company will focus on providing cards to every major social networking site currently on the market and on creating apps that will run on any media chosen by the consumer. While these efforts will be primarily focused initially only in the United States, long-term distribution goals include making our e-cards available internationally into the Canadian, European, Asian, and Latin American markets. Future plans include the creation of e-card kiosk stations that can be set up in specialty stores nationwide.

2. Advertising and Publicity

i. Advertising

Initially, we will rely heavily on our distribution strategy to put our product in the consumers' mind. For smaller companies in the greeting card industry, advertising in traditional media such as television and radio usually takes a back seat to distribution strategies. Moreover, except for sporadic commercials here and there, the larger companies of the industry rarely if ever advertise.

In the greeting card industry, a company's presence is known more so by where its products can be found rather than by elaborate advertising schemes. Word-of-mouth referrals are priceless and will easily cause recognition of our product to spread throughout the market, thereby enabling us to obtain our market share. The extent to which we intend to advertise initially will be determined through the efforts of our publicist.

ii. Publicity

In lieu of expending countless dollars on advertising campaigns and schemes, our company will enlist the services of a publicist who will promote the image of the company as well as help the company to gain exposure in the market and beyond. The publicist will use vehicles such as articles in various business and consumer magazines and any other magazine or newspaper that reaches our target audience.

Among other services, our publicist will organize charitable events that will not only mark the presentation of a new line of e-cards but will also serve to benefit one or several charitable organizations or educational institutions. Special guests and speakers will reflect some relationship to the new line of product.

COMPETITIVE ANALYSIS

Our competitors currently have a tight grasp on the traditional greeting card market. Nevertheless, their lines of e-cards are such that they warrant being called potential competitors.

Currently, the big greeting card companies are known for their Seasonal and Everyday lines of cards. They provide the average buyer all that is needed by way of birthday cards and "I love you" sentiments. These sentiments, while loving in nature, fail to serve those customers whose needs go far beyond simply saying "I love you" in a poetic way.

That's where we expect to leave the competition behind. Our potential competitors have yet to offer the technologically superior, creative platform for expressing a personalized message in the context of e-cards. Our product and distribution strategy sets us apart from the crowd. A typical e-card site is filled with thousands of cards to click on. The variety can be good yet overwhelming to the buyer. Our e-cards are less likely to be lost in the shuffle of a typical e-card site, crowded with greeting cards all competing for the consumers' attention. Thus, alternative distribution channels help us to compete and to rapidly gain customer recognition as being the company that they associate with this distinct kind of e-card.

ORGANIZATIONAL PLAN

a. CEO/President

As an incorporated entity, the founding principles of ABC E-Card Company will hold the top two offices of the corporation. This provides an effective means of checks and balances and keeps our original spirit of partnership alive. With degrees in both Computer Graphic Design and Film, the owners are well positioned to lead the company into the future of the e-card industry.

1. Chief Executive Officer

This office is responsible for nationwide operations affecting the product and product marketing. Thus, at all times, this office shall be responsible for determining the overall direction of the company and its products.

2. President

This office has the responsibility of directing and overseeing the day-to-day operations of the company, which includes all policy-making decisions based thereon.

b. Vice Presidents

For our company, the most important aspects of the company lie with the product; creating and developing the product, making the product, selling the product, and then distributing the product. The following three key positions will be held by designees of the founding principles.

1. Vice President of Creative Development

Reporting directly to the CEO, this officer's responsibilities include creating and developing ideas for new and existing lines of e-cards as well as new product in general. Responsibilities also include developing release time tables for each new line, overseeing and managing the research, creation and development process, and ensuring that the overall process stays within the prescribed time table for release.

2. Vice President of Operations

Reporting directly to the president, this officer's responsibilities include overseeing and managing all aspects of purchasing, production and distribution, which include inventory control, quality assurance, and production operations and activities. Responsibilities further include the continuous development of cost-effective, efficient methods of production and distribution.

3. Vice President of Sales

Reporting directly to the CEO, this officer's responsibilities include overseeing the acquisition of large and small e-store accounts, which consists of product presentation and closure of sales. This officer's responsibilities include overseeing and managing in-house account coordinators and online and mobile sales representatives. To the extent that independent contractor sales representatives are used, this officer will also be responsible for engaging, overseeing, and reporting on their efforts as well. Responsibilities further include collaboration with the company's marketing department to properly develop a sales strategy for international sales and distribution.

OPERATING PLAN

The following constitutes the entire operating plan for our company.

A. Customer Service Department

This department will be responsible for servicing our new and existing customers by answering questions and concerns relating to specific account inquiries as well as general questions about company policies and procedures as they relate to the customer/company relationship. This department will also send company brochures and catalogs upon request by prospective new accounts.

B. Purchasing Department

This department will be responsible for all company purchases as they relate to product and/or office equipment and supplies. This department shall also be responsible for directing proper records of all purchasing invoices to the appropriate accounting department while maintaining copies of same. Further responsibilities of this department include maintaining proper records regarding the servicing requirements on all office equipment as well as ensuring proper servicing of equipment when necessary.

C. Production/Distribution Department

This department will be responsible for overseeing all production and development of the e-cards and ensuring that each line is uploaded to account sites in a timely manner. Thus, the function of this department is to coordinate the actual production and distribution of the product.

D. Creative Development Department

This department will be responsible for the research, creation, and development of new lines and products for the company as well as the researching and development of additional material for existing lines.

E. Accounting Department

This department will be responsible for all accounts receivable and payable record keeping for online and mobile accounts and the company in general. Past-due notices will be generated from this department as well as the implementation of collection procedures.

F. Sales Department

This department is responsible for the acquisition of small and large online and mobile accounts. Responsibilities also include updating each account on our newest additions in e-card lines, product, and the like. This department will work in conjunction with the accounting department when running credit background checks on perspective new accounts. Upon acquiring the account, this department will forward the proper paperwork pertaining to the newly acquired account to the ordering department for processing, as well as the accounting department, in order to advise on the account's new status.

G. PR/Marketing Department

The PR/marketing department is responsible for managing the company's online presence including all company-owned websites and e-stores as well as overseeing all outsourced PR activities.

H. Administration Department

The accounting department, human resources, and any in-house legal team will eventually make up this department, thereby becoming departments within a department.

FINANCIAL PLAN

The initial capitalization required for this company is $35,000.00. ABC E-Card Company is seeking total financing from friends and family in addition to use of personal savings. Potential investors are advised to consider the following when determining a proposed investment (debt and/or equity) in this company:

1   The Company
ABC E-Card Company is a California closely held corporation electing S-Corp status for federal taxation purposes. This company relies heavily on the financial assistance and services of factoring companies, which pay on invoices, less a specified service fee percentage. This company will allocate ten percent (10%) of its' gross proceeds to a homeless organization of its choosing as an annual charitable contribution.

2.   Issuance of Securities
This corporation is authorized to issue only one class of shares of stock, which is designated "Common Stock." All shareholders shall be given one vote per share (i.e., if you own one hundred shares, you may cast one hundred votes for or against a shareholder action). The total number of shares that ABC is authorized to issue is ten thousand shares. Shares are priced at $30.00 per share. This issuance of securities shall be subject to and made in compliance with the Federal Private Offering Exemption contained in Section 4(2) of the Federal Securities Act, Regulation D Rule 506. Issuance of shares is further conditioned upon completion of a "Shareholder Representation Letter."

3.   Payment of Dividends
The payment of dividends shall be made in accordance with California Corporations Code section 500 et seq.

4. Loans (Credit Card Access)

   Access includes but is not limited to the option to maintain a monthly balance paying only the minimum monthly payment. Access also includes the option, without penalty, to pay all or part of the principle and any applicable finance charges at any time. Access to the full amount of the specified credit limit shall be made available at all times. Notwithstanding the foregoing, nothing herein shall obligate ABC E-Card Company to make use of the credit card as a means by which to capitalize the company.

5. Loan Repayment (Cash and Credit Card Loans)

   For loans originating from a credit card, ABC E-Card Company shall pay fifteen (15) percent interest on the total amount loaned plus repayment of credit card principle and any finance charges. For all other loans, ABC E-Card Company shall pay fifteen (15) percent interest on the total amount loaned plus repayment of principle. Repayment shall be triggered by the acquisition of an online or mobile account.

CONTINGENCY PLAN

The top four risks that our company may be exposed to follow below, as well as the solution that we feel minimizes the potential risks.

1. Product acceptance by consumers: Based upon the survey commissioned by ABC E-Card Company, we feel that consumer acceptance will be high and will therefore present minimal risk.

2. Production delays: Using back-up developers will greatly reduce this risk as well as completing the first line prior to soliciting initial online and mobile accounts.

3. Inability to obtain desired online and mobile account distribution channels: By researching and observing the buying tendencies of our desired online and mobile distributors, we feel that our product falls in line with the unique types of products that our desired distributors buy. Therefore, we feel that the risks of nonacceptance are minimal.

4. Increased competition from major competitors: Most of the larger card companies are already in the process of developing their own e-card lines. The risk of increased competition will be reduced through proprietary patents, superior product quality and product association of this company among consumers as the first e-card company to introduce this personalized product line.

Insert Appendix, including applicable
charts, graphs, and spreadsheets here.

Licensing and Permit Requirements

Depending on the state in which you reside, there may be licensing and permit requirements for starting your business. The following resource lists the relevant website addresses, by state, which contain business information concerning these licensing and permit requirements. While the information found on these sites may not represent a complete and comprehensive source with respect to all state, county, city or local requirements, it should serve as a helpful starting point for your new business research.

- Alabama
http://www.ador.state.al.us/licenses/index.html
- Alaska
http://www.commerce.state.ak.us/CBP/
- Arizona
http://www.azdor.gov/Business/LicensingGuide.aspx
- Arkansas
http://portal.arkansas.gov/business/Pages/businessCenter.aspx
- California
http://www.calgold.ca.gov/
- Colorado
http://www.dora.state.co.us/licensing.htm
- Connecticut
http://www.ct-clic.com/
- Delaware
https://onestop.delaware.gov/osbrlpublic/Home.jsp
- District of Columbia
http://dcra.dc.gov/DC/DCRA
- Florida
http://www.myflorida.com/taxonomy/business/

•Georgia
http://www.georgia.gov/00/
channel_title/0,2094,4802_5039,00.html
•Guam
http://www.investguam.com/index.
php?pg=license
•Hawaii
http://hawaii.gov/dbedt/business/start_grow/
Document.2005-10-13.4537
•Idaho
http://www.state.id.us/business/licensing.html
•Illinois
http://www2.illinois.gov/business/Pages/
default.aspx
•Indiana
http://www.state.in.us/ai/licensing/
•Iowa
http://www.iowalifechanging.com/
business/blic.aspx
•Kansas
http://www.kansas.gov/services/
•Kentucky
http://www.thinkkentucky.com/BIC/
ebpermits.aspx
•Louisiana
http://www.sos.louisiana.gov/tabid/98/
Default.aspx
•Maine
http://www.maine.gov/portal/business/
licensing.html
•Maryland
http://www.dat.state.md.us/sdatweb/tralicen.html
•Massachusetts
http://www.mass.gov/?pageID=mg2constituent&L
=2&L0=Home&L1=Business&sid=massgov2
•Michigan
http://www.michigan.gov/statelicensesearch

•Minnesota
http://www.license.mn.gov/
•Mississippi
http://www.mississippi.gov/ms_sub_sub_template.
jsp?Category_ID=20
•Missouri
http://www.business.mo.gov/register.asp
•Montana
http://bsd.dli.mt.gov/index.asp
•Nebraska
https://www.nebraska.gov/osbr/index.cgi
•Nevada
http://nvsos.gov/index.aspx?page=419
•New Hampshire
http://www.nh.gov/business/doingbusiness.html
•New Jersey
http://www.nj.gov/njbusiness/licenses/
•New Mexico
http://www.rld.state.nm.us/index.html
•New York
http://www.nys-permits.org/
•North Carolina
http://thrivenc.com/smallbusiness/
licensing-and-permitting
•North Dakota
http://www.nd.gov/businessreg/license/index.html
•Ohio
http://business.ohio.gov/licensing/
•Oklahoma
http://www.okcommerce.gov/sbrs/
•Oregon
http://licenseinfo.oregon.gov/
•Pennsylvania
http://www.newpa.com/build-your-business/
start/expert-assistance/center-for-entrepreneurial-
assistance

- Puerto Rico
http://www2.pr.gov/Pages/default.aspx
- Rhode Island
http://www.ri.gov/business/index.
php?subcategory=17&linkgroup=75
- South Carolina
http://sc.gov/business/Pages/
LICENSESANDPERMITSBUSINESS.aspx
- South Dakota
http://sd.gov/usefullinks_main.aspx
- Tennessee
http://www.tn.gov/topics/Business
- Texas
http://governor.state.tx.us/ecodev/
business_resources/sba/
- U.S. Virgin Islands
http://www.usvichamber.com/business_steps.htm
- Utah
http://www.dopl.utah.gov/licensing/index.html
- Vermont
http://www.vermont.gov/portal/business/
- Virginia
https://apps.cao.virginia.gov/IDC/index.html
- Washington
http://www.dol.wa.gov/business/
- West Virginia
http://www.business4wv.com/b4wvpublic/default.
aspx?pagename=startbusiness
- Wisconsin
http://www.wisconsin.gov/state/core/business.
html
- Wyoming
http://www.wyoming.gov/business.aspx